# The
# Tranquil
# Home

# The Tranquil Home

Mickey Baskett

## Sterling Publishing Co., Inc.
### New York

## Prolific Impressions Production Staff:

Editor in Chief: Mickey Baskett
Graphics: Dianne Miller, Karen Turpin
Styling: Kirsten Jones
Photography: Jerry Mucklow, David Bjurstrom, John Toth
Administration: Jim Baskett

10 9 8 7 6 5 4 3 2 1
Published by Sterling Publishing Co., Inc.
387 Park Avenue South, New York, N.Y. 10016
© 2003 by Prolific Impressions, Inc.
Produced by Prolific Impressions, Inc.
160 South Candler St., Decatur, GA 30030

Distributed in Canada by Sterling Publishing
c/o Canadian Manda Group, One Atlantic Avenue, Suite 105
Toronto, Ontario, Canada M6K 3E7
Distributed in Great Britain by Chrysalis Books
64 Brewery Road, London N7 9NT, England
Distributed in Australia by Capricorn Link (Australia) Pty. Ltd.
P.O. Box 704, Windsor, NSW 2756 Australia
Printed in China
All rights reserved
Sterling ISBN  0-8069-7101-0

## Acknowledgements

- Stanton Designs, E. Ponce de Leon, Decatur, GA, which allowed us to photograph the beautiful living spaces in their shop that sells Asian influenced furniture and accessories, plus candles and bath products.

- Whispering Waters Bed & Breakfast, Traverse City, MI (www.whisperingwaters.com) which allowed us to share the woodsy elegance of their retreat.

- Lorrie Cook, an interior decorator from Pierce & Parker in St. Simons, GA who allowed us to photograph her home as well as other homes she has decorated.

- Marie Browning who shared her expertise in working with vellum and parchment. See Marie's book, *Crafting with Vellum and Parchment* published by Sterling Publications for more wonderful projects.

- Plaid Enterprises, Inc., www.plaidonline.com, for home décor painting and other products used to create projects and room settings – Stencil Décor stencils and paints; FolkArt® Acrylic Colors, Crackle Medium, and sealers; All Night Media® Rubber Stamps; Decorator Products™ Block Print Stamp and glazes.

- Yaley Enterprises, www.yaley.com, for supplies used for candlemaking (Candle Crafting), soap-making (Soapsations™), and other bath products.

- Fountain Magic, www.fountain-magic.net, for a complete line of fountain pumps and fountain making accessories.

# The Tranquil Home

## Table of Contents

# Introduction

We seek serenity. In today's frenetic techno workplaces, we need a balance. We need a home that can be a refuge, our sanctuary – a place to take a deep breath, focus inward, and to feel the calm. This book offers you ways to make that happen. From page after page of beautiful room examples to projects you can make for your home – this book is filled with ways to help you create a tranquil living space for you and your family.

What makes a home tranquil? Answering this question is the heart of this book.

A tranquil home, is not just a home with a monochromatic color scheme. It goes deeper than that. The theory espoused in this book is that a tranquil home contains all the earth's natural elements in balance – wood, fire, earth, water, and metal. When your décor

On this well organized and inviting desk, modern technology is balanced by the antique calendar from 1910 and other antique printed matter. The poem, bible verse, and art remind us of beauty that nature passes on from generation to generation. Today's stresses are less than a blink in time.

contains all natural elements in balance you will feel at peace and harmony with your surroundings. This may be an Asian idea – but your home does not have to have an Asian décor to be able to use these principles. This book offers you ideas for introducing earth's elements into your home – for all styles of home decorating. Examples of colors and lists of items that represent each element are included. Then ways to use those items are shown in room photos and project examples. By using nature as a guide, combined with a few rules for good design, you can learn how to create a room that is tranquil, serene, and stylish.

Not only does this book include photos of rooms to use as examples, but it also includes many projects that can be made to help you create a more tranquil atmosphere. A sampling of projects included follows:

• Easy fountains to make

• Making candles and parchment lanterns

• Furniture decorated with designs from nature such as stenciled fern

• Mosaic projects

• How to use plants and flowers in decorating

• Aromatherapy guidelines

• Making a buckwheat and lavender relaxation pillow

• Creating a windchime garden stake

# Nature's Five Elements

In traditional Western thought, the earth is made up of four elements: Fire, Earth, Air, and Water. The concept of Five Elements – Wood, Fire, Earth, Metal, and Water – has it roots in Chinese thought. It is one of the pillars on which traditional Chinese Medicine was built – but these principles can be used in the home environment. In this theory, there are five elements and their energies effect one another by creating or destroying one another. And all known phenomena – everything in nature – can be classified by how their properties match those of earth's Five Elements. Whether it is colors, tastes, weather, or feelings – the Chinese have categorized these phenomena under one of the Five Element categories. By doing this, they can establish their relationship and mutual interaction.

Everything in nature is related and affects something else in nature. For example, we water a plant (in the wood category) to make it grow; thus, water promotes wood. Wood burns easily, giving rise to fire. Fire leaves ashes which are categorized as an earth element. Ashes go back to the earth and become part of the layers. Metals are mined within the earth. Here each element promotes or creates the other. But each can also destroy the other. Plants (or wood) can destroy earth by depleting it of nutrients. A metal axe can destroy the wood. A fire can melt the metal axe. Water can put out the fire. The flow of water can be stopped by the earth.

This creation and destruction is the natural order of growth and development and keeps the elements balanced and in check. The problem comes when the elements are out of balance. If the fire is too big it may not be able to be controlled by water. Or a river may swell so much that the banks of earth may not be able to control its flow.

The Five Elements are also associated with direction, and the direction of the flowing energy each element possesses. You can imagine this energy by thinking about the season that each element represents. In the spring,

plants are breaking through the earth, trees are budding out and reaching upwards toward the sun – the energy of the Wood element is flowing upwards. For the Fire element, picture the middle of a hot summer day when everything is in full bloom and the sun's energy is expanding in every direction. The Earth element is represented by early autumn when the leaves begin to change color and fall as the sun gets lower in the sky. Metal is represented by late autumn when all energy seems to be moving inward and preparing for winter. In winter (the Water element) the surface is hard and quiet, yet the energy is flowing underneath, preparing to be awakened soon.

We can use nature and the energy of its elements to help us attain balance and harmony in our homes. By introducing natural elements into our homes from the five elements, we can establish a serene environment, one that will promote the growth and development of our family life. We can create a home full of life and vitality that links us to our surroundings. Relax, there are no hard and fast rules about how you should combine these elements to create harmony in your home. The most important guideline is that your décor should suit your lifestyle and your personality. And don't be afraid to change your concepts about your environment – the world changes and so do the rules.

Rooms can overwhelmingly represent one element but still be in balance and tranquil to some personalities and out of balance with others. A room with too much Metal is disconcerting to some personalities while one with too much Wood energy makes another overwhelmed. Too much Water energy in one room has the effect of "going with the flow" or being "wishy-washy" and not being able to make a decision. Depending upon your personality and what you are trying to achieve in a room, you can use the knowledge of the characteristics of each element to bring in the type of energy you wish to each room. You can enhance or stimulate with

some Fire elements, or calm a room with Water elements. You may want a very calm bedroom using lots of Water or Earth elements – while in your living room you may wish to use Fire elements to promote sociability or Wood elements to promote activity. An office would be a good choice for using Wood and Metal elements while a family room would be very cozy and enjoyable with Earth elements.

Using nature's elements in our home does not dictate a particular style of décor to our home. Using some of the Five Elements principles does not mean that you need to decorate with an Asian influence. Any decorating style can still embody the Five Elements. For example, in a traditional decorating style, a hardwood floor represents the Wood element and grounds you; a gold leafed mirror can be used to introduce both Fire and Water; a brass bowl for the Metal element filled with cinnamon sticks and other spicy potpourri items for the Earth element is another example of introducing and balancing the various elements in a room.

On the following pages are lists of items that have been traditionally linked with each of the Five Elements. Even colors and climate can be charted under one of the elements. You can introduce the Five Elements into your decorating in the form of building materials, furnishings, and decorating accessories. The energy that flows through these items can subtly affect our minds and bodies – causing us to think and act differently. Use these lists

to help you choose items from each category to decorate your rooms for optimal effects. Create an environment that will enhance and nourish your life. When you can bring nature into your home by using wood, earth, fire, metal, and water, you can create a balance that will bring tranquility to your home.

A fat, laughing Buddha is a Chinese symbol of wealth. Invite him into your home to bring you success. Place him facing the front door for maximum effect.

# Wood

# Characteristics of Wood Elements

A room with mostly Wood elements is stimulating and helps concentration and activity. A young person, a person with lack of confidence or drive would benefit from being in a Wood element room; while a workaholic might be over stimulated. A room with green-colored wall and lots of wood furniture and books is a perfect environment for a busy office.

**Season** - Spring, a time for growth and the sprouting of new leaves.
**Color** - Green
**Shapes** - Vertical, thin, tall
**Direction** - Up, moving upwards
**Characteristic** - Growth, development, vitality
**Promotes** - Activity, being busy, ambition, career

**Items to Use in Your Environment:**

Wood furniture

Books arranged uniformly

Green Plants

Bamboo

Jute, sisal, hemp

Paper, journals

Bark

Tall wooden containers

Tall plants

Flowers (fresh) to energize your space

Fruit

Tea

High shelves to create rising energy

Split cane blinds

Handmade paper lampshades

*Continued on page 18*

17

*Continued from page 16*

Baskets

Framed pressed flowers or fern

Fabrics derived from plants such as cotton and linen (excluding wool and silk)

Display of green apples

Carved wooden architectural elements

Cane tables or chairs

Palm trees

Ferns

Acanthus leaf symbol

Wallpaper with vertical stripes

Nature elements stenciled on walls

Twisted branches and vines

Using baskets as containers to organize pantries or shelves.

*Pictured above and right:* The Whispering Waters Bed and Breakfast in Traverse City, Michigan showcases artful furniture and architectural elements that were made from the wood found on the property. This certainly links the inside to the outside in a most elemental way. Shown in the photo above, the stair railings were constructed from peeled branches that are both functional as well as beautifully artful. Shown opposite, a table and a mirror uses birch peelings as well as willow twigs for their design.

# Fire

A room where you have parties or want to promote passion and expression are the rooms where you want to use many Fire elements. A conference room that is used to brainstorm new ideas would benefit from using the colors red and exhibiting pointed or star shaped items. These types of rooms are not good for relaxation.

# Characteristics of Fire Element

**Season** - Summer
**Colors** - Red, orange
**Shapes** - Pointed, triangular, pyramid
**Direction** - All directions, radiating outward
**Characteristic** - Passion, warmth, excitement
**Promotes** - Passion, parties, sociability, spontaneity, new ideas

### Items to Use in Your Environment:

Gold Leafing

Sunlight

Sun motifs or sun shapes

Star printed wallpaper

Star shapes

Chimineas

Lumineria

Fireplaces

Lighting

Oil lamps

Candles to add energy

Pyramid or pointed containers

Incense to clear the atmosphere

Crystals

Bright colored silk cushions

Sunflower pattern

Heart-shaped elements

Hang a prism in the window to introduce fiery flashes of light

# Earth

A very earthy room feels like home. The elements associated here promote the feelings of stability, caring, and security. For a new family, decorating in an earthy style could enhance family harmony. A room with tile floors, checked fabric on the low comfortable sofas and chairs, and surrounded with ochre walls would be perfect for a family great room – yet not at all appropriate for a first office or an art studio.

There are many things that are symbolic of the earth's energy. Rounded shapes represent the curve of the earth, giving items the appearance of stability. Clay items bring us down to earth by giving us the feeling of security. A collection of pebbles or rocks will give you a sense of connection to the earth. Earth elements help you remember where you have come from and perhaps give you a vision of where you are going. You can honor remembrance by having a collection of photos of family members.

# Characteristics of Earth Element

**Season** - Late Summer or early Autumn, mediates changes between the seasons
**Colors** - Brown, yellow
**Shapes** - Wide, horizontal, low, flat
**Direction** - Downward
**Characteristic** - Centered, nurturing, resourceful, comfort
**Promotes** - Family harmony, security, stability, motherhood

### Items to Use in Your Environment:

Terra cotta tiles help us stay grounded

Mosaics

Sand

Porcelain

China

Clay

Pottery

Crystal

Plaster

Bricks

Paint pigments

Horizontal or checked patterns on walls and fabrics

Rounded forms

Low clay containers or bowls

Checked fabric

Velvet

Suede

Root vegetables

Stepping stones

Pumpkins and gourds

Spices

Salt to remove negativity

Aromatherapy fragrances of cedar, sandalwood, oranges

# Metal

Introducing the Metal element can help to create an uncluttered look, creating focus and organization to your lifestyle. With the characteristic of clean, simple lines, Metal helps relax the mind and gives a sense of direction or purpose.

# Characteristics of Metal Element

**Season** - late Autumn
**Colors** - Pale colors of white, silver, gold
**Shapes** - Round, domed, spherical
**Direction** - Moving inward, becoming solid
**Characteristic** - Ordered, structured, leadership
**Promotes** - Organization, finances, business, planning ahead

**Items to Use in Your Environment:**

Metal pots for plants

Silver & gold leafing

Gemstones

Iron

Silver

Stainless steel

Spherical metal shapes

Round metal pots

Wire trays and forms

Money, coins to invite prosperity into your life

Lime wash on wood

Copper or brass vases

Hard, shiny stone such as marble and granite

Metal windchimes to help you focus and slow down the flow of
energy

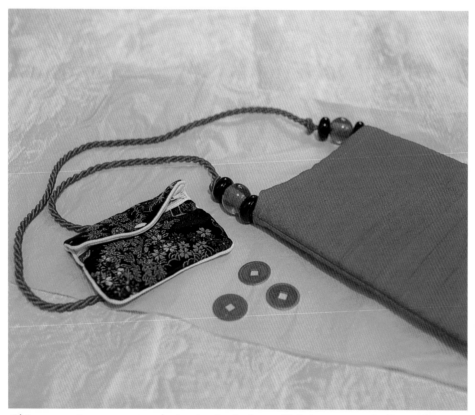

Chinese coins are not only intriguingly beautiful, but many believe that
they promote a healthy income. Three coins ( a symbolic number) placed
in your wallet or handbag can symbolize and acknowledge wealth-luck.
The Chinese believe it is very important to tie these three coins with a red
cord or ribbon to activate the energy.

# Water

A single perfect blossom in a pool of pebbles inspires thoughts of tranquility. The rippling moiré fabric mimics the ripples of water on the pools surface.

Many types of rooms in the home will benefit by containing strong Water energy. A room decorated for an elderly person or someone convalescing should make use of items associated with the Water element because it is associated with healing and well-being. Water elements also promote sleep so a bedroom with a fountain or a fish bowl on the night stand would ensure a good night's rest. And since Water is also a symbol for affection and sexuality – a marriage bedroom is the perfect place for an aquarium.

**Season** - Winter
**Colors** - Blue, pearl, black, iridescent & reflecting
**Shapes** - Curved, wavy, irregular
**Direction** - Flowing below the surface
**Characteristic** - Contemplation, quiet, sexuality, depth, tranquility
**Promotes** - Spirituality, tranquility, sexual activity, sleep, conception

**Items to Choose for Decorating:**

Aquariums

Mirror

Glass

Satin and moiré

Shells

Curved glass vases

Wavy lines

Swirly shapes

Natural bath products to cleanse

Desk top fountains add a soothing sound to a room

Fish bowls add life and serenity

A well ordered bathroom can create a haven for relaxation

# Harmonious Decorating

## A Portrait in Ivory

A living room is at the heart of most family spaces. It needs to be relaxing and comfortable, yet at the same time promote sociability and harmony. The seating pieces should be soft with rounded shapes and should be arranged to promote communication. The cream color used in the seating pieces shown is a calming color. Here curtains help to slow the energy and add a relaxing effect – yet are pulled back to allow the sunlight to energize the room. The wall color promotes the relaxing, spacious feeling. The tall plants with their upward energy and stacks of books introduce life and vitality into this sedate room.

## Seaside Living

Light, airy, uncluttered rooms are desirable for home harmony. The combination of pale colors, natural wood and natural fabrics produce a relaxed atmosphere. The soft upholstery is soothing. However, there are some uplifting touches in the room to give it life – candles burning for the Fire element, a reflective glass tabletop for the Water element

## Exotic
## Guest Room

This room is energized with Fire and Wood. The fiery red/orange walls are tempered somewhat by the blue ocean in the framed world maps and the creamy silk curtains. The touches of metal add a sleek structure to the room. This is an exciting, beautiful room for guests. Even though the room is small, it doesn't feel cramped, but feels cozy. The rich wall color creates that warm feeling, and the minimal and unobtrusive window treatments allow plenty of air and light to enter the room.

41

## Traditional Comfort

This room is filled with harmonious furnishings. The shape of the furniture you choose and the materials it is made with affect the balance of energy in the room. Rounded shapes, soft upholstered pieces, and furniture made from wood have a calming effect. Hard shiny materials such as the marble floor – and angular shapes such as the square tables add stimulation, creating a balance in the room.

## Sleeping in Grand Style

This bedroom is a cozy retreat, containing accessories to represent every element. The green of the walls and the cane furniture represents the Wood element making the room lively, uplifting and cheerful. The color orange and the gold leafed frame bring in a bit of Fire, aiding romance and passion. The iron bed brings the Metal element – adding structure and solidity. Water is represented by the silky fabric of the bedspread, the reflecting glass of the framed pictures. The earthy colors used on the bedspread make the bed seem secure and comfortable.

Things to consider to create a comfortable bedroom are:

- Lighting – Lamps are better than overhead lights because the shades help diffuse the harshness. Candles are a romantic addition to the bedroom.
- Storage – Plenty of wardrobe space will eliminate disconcerting clutter.
- Bed Linens – Natural fiber bed coverings of cotton, linen, or silk are best . Thread count of the linens is important for feel – stay above 220 thread count for a luxurious feel. Don't leave your bed unmade during the day. Have plenty of pillows for support. Avoid synthetic fabrics.
- Furniture – soft rounded forms are more comforting. Wood and wicker are made from softer material and more tranquil.
- Floor – Wall to wall carpeting creates a uniform and relaxing atmosphere – so it is ideal for use in a bedroom.
- Drapery – Full draped windows help soften noises and slow down the energy in a room. Drapery should be pulled closed at night for a more restful sleep.
- Accessories – Placing items such as pictures in pairs suggests intimacy. Notice the pair of birds above the bed in this room, and the pair of slipper chairs.

# Room
# With a View

Soft muted colors in this room make it ultra relaxing. This room has all the components of a comfortable bedroom – soft and comfortable bedding; a wooden bedframe; pairs of objects to symbolize closeness; drapery that can be pulled shut; storage space; uniform fitted carpeting; calming colors.

If you wish to create an atmosphere of romance in a bedroom there are objects and colors you can choose to assure this. Red and purple are the colors of romance. If you don't wish to paint your walls these colors, you can use the colors in small doses. A vase of red or purple flowers, purple candles, or a painting with touches of purple or red will be fine. Displaying objects in pairs helps to enhance close relationships – pictures, lamps, chairs, etc. Candles are the ultimate romantic element because they increase Fire energy which promotes passion. A pair of candlesticks or a pair of candles would be a wonderful romantic accessory. Your goal is to create a nest-like atmosphere that is protective, secure, comfortable, attractive, and intimate. That's a tall order – but it is possible when you consider the principles associated with the five elements.

# Cozy Dining

It is important to set aside a special place where your family can have meals together. Our lives are so hectic that it is even more essential to make that effort to share time and food together. A pleasant atmosphere for dining will help everyone relax and aid in digestion. The seating arrangement and the tabletop display should be conducive to conversation. When designing your family dining space, consider colors, materials used for the table-top surface and chairs, plants, and linens.

This dining room has the essentials for harmonious and relaxing family dining. The color scheme used is great for family gatherings because

white promotes relaxation while blue promotes communication. The natural wood and rush chairs are soft materials that have a calming effect – as do the decorative wall baskets. The white of the placemats and napkins coupled with the crispness of the fabric enhances the concept of cleanliness – an essential element to enjoying a meal.

The roundness of the flower arrangement is calming while the bright green adds life. A cloth on the table helps cut sound and the energy in a room – using a natural fiber in the cloth is essential. The open shelving displaying antique pieces adds a note of stability, history, and security to the setting.

## A Grand Rest

The décor of this bedroom was designed as an intimate space for a married couple. The neutral colors used for the walls, the floor covering, the upholstered pieces, and the bed linens have a calming effect. The rounded forms seen throughout the room increase notions of sensuality and also are very soothing. Notice the rounded and soft form of the sofa; the round and swirling bedpost design; the shape of the headboard; the round lampbase shapes; the rounded shapes in the wall pieces above the bed. Pairs of objects also increase the intimacy of the relationship – lamps, sculptures, matching bedside chests. Natural fiber fabrics for the bed covering and bed linens are essential for comfort. The drapery is neutral and can be pulled to cover the window, shutting out light and creating a secure feeling.

## Bathing
## in
## Luxury

A large bathroom with lots of light as the one shown here is preferable and energizing. An inside bathroom without access to sunlight or fresh air is the least desirable type of bathroom, making the space feel damp, heavy, and stagnant. This room possesses many Earth elements such as the wall color, the natural marble, the rounded shapes – giving the space a secure, comforting ambiance. The Wood elements bring vitality to the space, guarding against boredom – notice the plants, the tall lamps, wooden furnishings and curtain rods. The Fire element is introduced with the lamps, sunlight, and touches of red. The Water element is naturally represented in any bathroom – yet the uneven flowing pattern and the shiny surface of the marble also provide the water influence. Metal is represented with the fixtures, imparting order and structure.

# A
# Nostalgic
# Corner

There should be a place set aside where you can display revered elements from your past. The corner of this bedroom is used for this purpose. Atop the sponge-painted cabinet is a grouping of things held dear by the inhabitant of the room. The antique boxes hold trinkets and pieces of whimsy that hold fond memories. The set of candle-sticks are a precious reminder of a dear ancestor. The man and woman statue is the figurine used atop parent's wedding cake.

## A Place for Meditation

This home owner has set aside a quiet, private place in his home for contemplation and meditation. The chair, with its rounded shape and natural fabric coverings, can be transformed into a bed for personal relaxation or to accommodate guests. Natural rush, jute, and bamboo that are used for the screen, tables, and other accessories have a hushing effect. On the low table is a fountain, symbolizing flowing energy and is the focus point for mediation sessions. The candle is used to help generate new ideas or new ways of thinking about things during times of contemplation. On the following two pages are closeups of these items.

The sitting area shown on this page and the one opposite use the principles of the Five Elements to create harmonious and comfortable living spaces.

## A Reading Retreat

Taking time for the enjoyment of reading is important to our well being. Having a comfortable space for this reading enhances the effect. This chair, covered in soft velvet with a soft, plump, rounded shape is perfect for relaxing. Good lighting is within arms reach. Storage space is available in the small chest to hold pencils, book marks, notepads. Everything in this room was chosen for its calming effect on the space. Even the rounded knobs on the chest have an effect on the calming energy. The plant, with its floppy leaves has downward energy, helping to promote concentration. The oxygen it provides is healthy and promotes well-being. The wood and reed furniture and accessories chosen have a relaxing result. A little bit of Fire is introduced in the form of pillow colors and a lamp so that the atmosphere does not get too stagnant and boring.

## Natural Space for Living

The materials, the positioning, and the design of the elements in this room all blend perfectly to create a harmonious living area. At Whispering Waters bed and breakfast, much attention is given to creating spaces where people can relax and reflect. Much of the time the property is used for group retreats that are energizing and healing. The space is not stagnant, but lively and designed for communication and conviviality. Yet there are spaces provided where one can retreat for personal time. The rooms possess items of all the five elements and they are used for maximum effect.

## Elegant
## Simplicity

Sparsely decorated with simple lines, this bedroom is comfortable and at the same time elegant, without being fussy. The linen fiber bed-coverings with the cotton throw quilt are natural fabrics that are durable and practical for bedroom use. The lace table covering and lace curtains bring a bit of femininity and pattern to an otherwise plain decorating scheme. The color red adds fire and romance to the room, while the plant adds life and oxygen for good health.

## Woodsy Appeal

This room is very appealing because of the muted colors and the natural fibers and materials used. The leaf printed bed linens set the theme of nature. The muted wall painting with a sponging effect gives the walls interest. The Wood energy comes from the furniture, books, and pussy willow stems. A bit of lively Fire energy is brought into the setting with the red crackled dresser top, and a candle. Water energy is introduced with the pearly dots on the wall.

The walls treatment was created by first painting the walls the neutral beige color. The stripes were then measured and taped off with painters masking tape. A glaze was created by mixing white paint with a clear glazing medium. This is available in many craft stores and home improvement stores. A natural sea sponge was used to pat the white glazing mixture on the masked off striped areas of the wall. In the beige striped sections, dots of iridescent paint were randomly dabbed on using a finger.

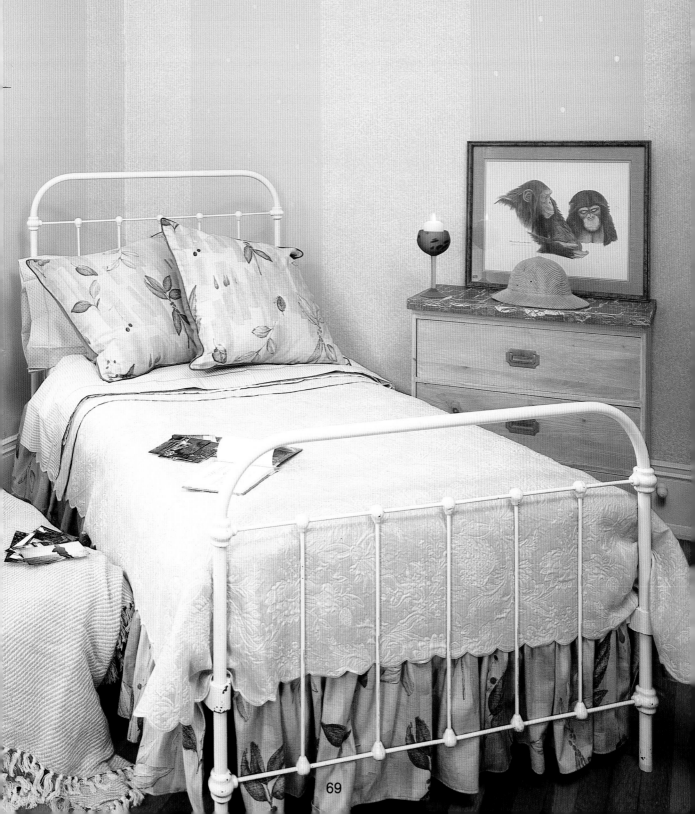

## Waterside Retreat

*Pictured left:* This room reflects the positioning of the house – on the shores of a large lake. The fluid white curtains and the blue and white color scheme are reminders of Water energy. Because the house is in the mountains rather than at the seashore, the wooden walls seem to anchor the house to the woodsy environment. The walls were stained with a white glaze (a mixture of white paint and a clear glazing medium) and the ceiling was stained with a blue glaze. The wooden bedhead is reminiscent of Adirondak chairs as seen in the print over the bed.

## A Country Retreat

*Pictured below:* This bedroom at the Whispering Waters bed and breakfast provides private space for romance as well as sociability and relaxation. The red walls and the red and neutral color of the bed linens inspire romance and vitality. Pairs of lamps and the symmetry of the room promote intimacy. Stability and comfort are increased by the Metal energy of the bed frame with its rounded form. A seating alcove with lots of windows to the outdoors is a break from the intensity of the bedroom space.

## Farmstead Home

A dining room/kitchen combination in this renovated farmhouse is a gathering place for the family. The fireplace seems to draw everyone in and encourage communication and sociability. Wood and Earth elements balance one another in this room to create a harmonious feeling. Metal plates and containers bring solidity to the room. Sometimes the energy introduced to represent an element can be very subtle, and possibly not even noticeable - yet we can instinctually feel the harmony and tranquility a room may possess. I often notice that a good decorator has the ability to balance a room – sometimes without even being conscious of the principles being practiced.

Although the Water element is not represented in this area of the room – it can be seen on the opposite side of the room where a corner cupboard displays a collection of cut glass; and the sink is central to the furnishings.

## Minimalist Tradition

Because this bedroom is furnished so simply, it gives us a feeling of order. The traditional theme that is strictly adhered to gives a sense of security, stability, and history to the room. Energy can flow freely in a room that is not cluttered. The wood furniture has the advantage of being easy to clean and creates a relaxing atmosphere without being boring. The bed linens add the proper softness to the room.

# Tranquility Helpers

• Use natural materials and fibers over artificial ones – cotton, linen, or down bedding; wool carpeting is preferable to nylon.

• Reduce clutter. Discard, sell, or give-away items you do not use – or absolutely love. Remove dust-catchers and be selective about the art you display. An organized room is tremendously calming.

• Living plants, animals, and people bring positive energy into your home.

• Live plants fill your home with life and healthy oxygen.

• Choose light and neutral colors and a monochromatic color scheme for the most calming effects.

• Air needs to move through your home and the sunshine needs to come in the window and cleanse the atmosphere.

• In each room of your home, the five elements (wood, fire, earth, metal, water) should be represented in some form – however small it might be. ❏

# Home Comforts

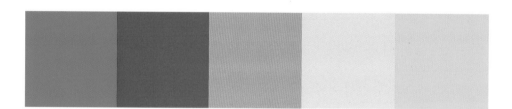

I have observed that the most comfortable homes are also the most stylish. Creating a home that is both comfortable and stylish is no easy task but it is possible. It is a balancing act between the things that make us feel relaxed and contented and the things that have a purpose, structure and contain those authoritative "rules" of good design. By using the five elements principles, some common sense about your family's needs, and good decorating standards, you can have the comfortable home you desire.

Making your home comfortable is an important element in the tranquility of a home. In our busy world, sometimes our homes are just places to change our clothes and get a night's sleep. Our homes should be our sanctuary. They should be a place that is comfortable, sacred and a place where our souls can be at home – and a place that will make us want to spend more time there. Following are some small steps you can take to add comfort to your home.

## The Quiet Hours

Time away from voices, from technology, from the sun; a minute to surround yourself in soft colors and soft fabrics; a moment to kick off your shoes, breathe a sigh while sipping a cup of rejuvenating tea – you owe yourself this. Carve out a corner for a chaise lounge that is all yours; a place where you can indulge in comfort and private thoughts – or better yet – no thoughts at all. Let the peace of the moment flow into you, then you can move back into the world feeling confident and relaxed.

## Comfort

By confining the palette of this bedroom to soft white and neutrals, a sense of space and calm prevails. Shades of linen and pure white maximize the light in the room. Swathed in vintage Parisian-style linens, organdy, and lace, the bed almost seems to float. Furniture pieces upholstered in natural linen and wood pieces painted white add the finishing touches. The room has a peaceful, airy mood.

## Porch Living

When you really want to relax, there is no better place than a comfortable porch. To be able to breathe in fresh air, feel a soft breeze and a bit of sun on your face, smell the heady aroma of blooming lilacs wafting by – this is a bit of porch heaven. The two porches pictured, though very different, are both stylish and appealingly comfortable. The first step to creating a comfortable porch is to find the right seating piece – a wicker sofa, a big roomy swing, an old-fashioned glider. Then load it up with plenty of soft pillows and bright gay fabrics. Add a few plants in pots, a chair or two, and a table to hold your lemonade – and you have it made in the shade.

## Books, Journals, Correspondence

Reading, writing in a journal, or corresponding with friends is necessarily a time of quiet. These tasks require that you focus, quiet your mind, and indulge in a little self-contemplation. All else seems to fade away as you get lost in the adventures of young Tom and his friend Huck; or as you put to paper your thoughts and feelings of the day; or perhaps you reminiscence in a note about the wonderful dinner you had at your friend's house.

Set aside a place in your home for reading, meditation, or writing. A place with a big comfortable seat, adequate light, a place that is isolated from the temptations of work or television; a place where you can let your stress dissolve. Please don't forget to make your place beautiful. Use natural fabrics for the chair, choose colors that soothe you, surround yourself with objects or designs from nature; make it a place that has the "ahh" factor.

There is something about a sturdy book, square and tactile, that speaks to the soul much better than a television or computer screen. It's easy to get annoyed at the computer or television. It's hard to get annoyed at a book if you have chosen the title wisely. Its touch to your fingers is soft as it grips your mind and sometimes your heart.

*Pictured below:* Book cases filled with treasured volumes, and stacks of books waiting to be opened and possessed – there is hardly anything that evokes a greater feeling of security and comfort than imagining yourself in a quiet spot with a beloved book.

*Pictured right:* Tranquility likes a view. Here this chair sits in perfect solitude overlooking the sea. This cottage with one room for reading and a sleeping loft above is the perfect place to escape to. Although it is just outside the backdoor of the main house, it takes its owner to far away places as she reads and dreams away a sunny afternoon. It's a playhouse for a weary mind.

A set of rubber stamps with Asian symbols are fun to use for creating your own notecards. Shown also is a handmade journal covered with marbleized paper. Asian symbol rubber stamps using embossing ink were used to decorate the cover.

# Relaxing Buckwheat and Lavender Pillow

Combine the best of two therapies - scent and sleep. Lavender has long been recognized as one of the most healing herbs in existence. It is believed that it can relax, comfort and soothe the most restless. Add lavender to a pre-sewn buckwheat pillow then place it into an attractive pillow cover to create a simple and beautiful pillow you can use. The buckwheat pillow can be slightly warmed to soothe your aches and release the wonderful calming lavender scent. The protective pillow cover you make is attractive and will keep your inner pillow clean. *Designed by Jean Henrich.*

*Instructions on page 94.*

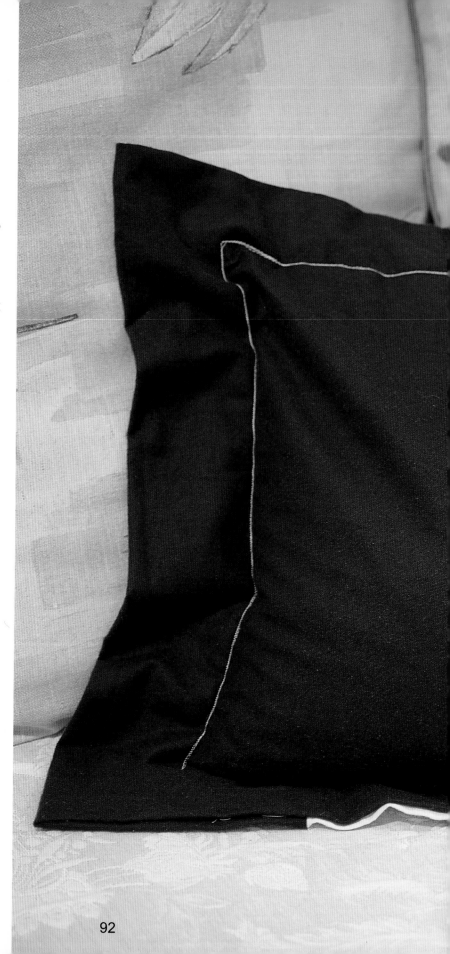

# Relaxing
# Buckwheat and Lavender
# Pillow

## Supplies

Premade buckwheat pillow (available at most drug stores)

2 pieces fabric, each 16" x 20" (muslin used)

1 piece fabric, 27" x 20" (blue cotton flannel used)

1 piece fabric, 6" x 6" (white felt used)

1 piece fabric, 3-1/2" x 6-1/2" for design (blue cotton flannel)

1 piece fabric, 4-1/2" x 7-1/2" for design (white wool felt)

1 piece of fabric, 3" x 5" for cutting out leaf design (white wool felt)

3 buttons

Matching thread and contrasting thread

Sewing machine

3 cups of dried lavender flowers

## Here's How

1. Carefully undo about 4-5" of one of the seams of the buckwheat pillow. Add 3 cups of lavender to the pillow, pouring into the undone seam. Sew the seam closed. Shake the pillow to disperse and blend the lavender and buckwheat.

2. Use the 16" x 20" pieces of fabric for the pillow back. On one 16" side of each piece fold over 1", then fold over 1" again. This will be the area to place the buttons and button holes. *See Fig. 1 and 2.*

3. At folded down areas, measure and mark 4" from each end. Space the buttons and the button holes within the center area. *See Fig. 3.*

4. Decorate the front piece (27" x 20" blue piece) with the leaf cutout and fabric squares. Use the leaf pattern given. *See Fig. 4.*

5. Place the front and back pieces together, right sides facing, and pin around edges. Sew together using 1/2" seam allowances. Leave an unsewn area for turning. *See Fig. 5.* Turn right side out and sew seam closed.

6. Topstitch around the edge of the pillow using a contrasting thread (white used) if desired. Stitch 2" in on longer sides and 2-1/2" in on shorter sides. *See Fig. 6.*

7. Insert the buckwheat and lavender pillow. ❑

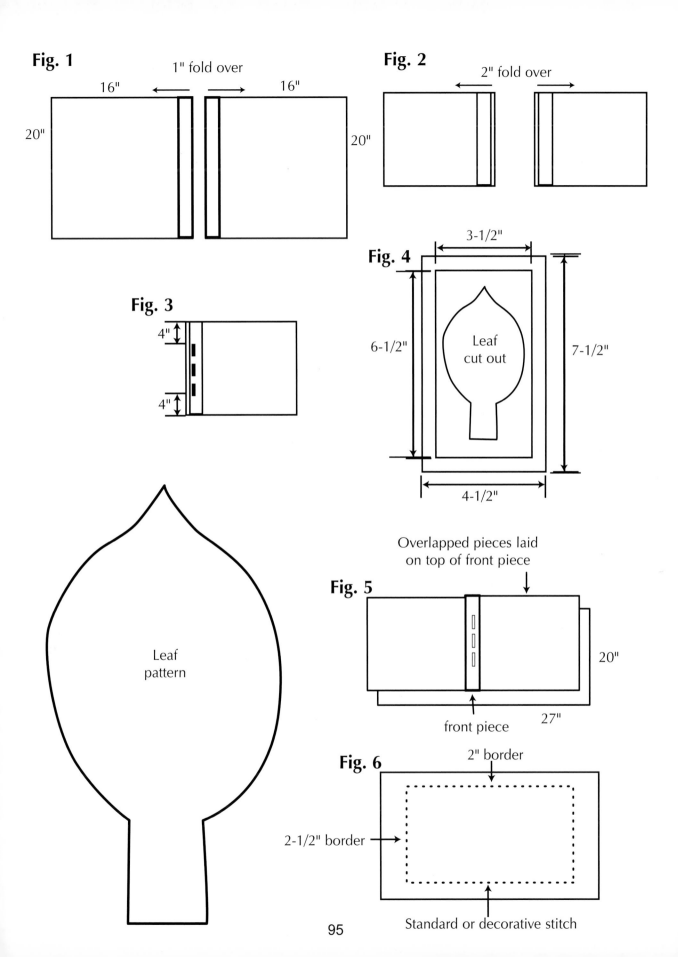

**Fig. 1**

1" fold over

16"    16"

20"    20"

**Fig. 2**

2" fold over

20"    20"

**Fig. 3**

4"

4"

**Fig. 4**

3-1/2"

6-1/2"    Leaf cut out    7-1/2"

4-1/2"

Leaf pattern

Overlapped pieces laid on top of front piece

**Fig. 5**

20"

front piece    27"

**Fig. 6**

2" border

2-1/2" border

Standard or decorative stitch

95

# Pleasures of Tea

Whether it is in the English tradition or Asian, taking time out to enjoy tea is an essential indulgence for a tranquil lifestyle. The time spent in the preparation and the partaking is soothing and calming. Not only can the time ritual and the taste be important, but also the smell and color is essential for sensory enjoyment.

Tea is a beverage made from the young leaves of a tea plant which is in the Camellia family. Tea leaves are fermented for different periods of time. The length of time is carefully chosen, for it will determine the tea's color, taste, aroma and character. A short fermentation brings green and yellow tones to the tea. Longer periods produce a red tea – and if also baked, a deep red strong tea will result. Logically, the most natural tasting teas (green teas) are not fermented and baked.

Primarily tea is a wonderful thirst quencher, an appetizer, and a good aid to digestion. It can also keep the breath fresh and is good for the teeth, helping to fight tooth decay. It is also believed to help fight hypertension, and calms the stomach. On the spiritual side, it relaxes and calms the nerves and reflects the tradition of hospitality and wisdom.

## Brewing Tea

**The temperature of the water** is very important. In general, use freshly boiled water, just off the stove for dark, strong teas. With lighter teas – such as green tea, pouchong, green oolong – let the boiled water cool for five minutes – let it cool to 176-194 degrees Fahrenheit, or 80-90 degrees Celsius.

**Quantity:** use an amount of tea that is equivalent to 2/5 of the size of the pot. This rule applies to all varieties of teas.

**When making a single cup,** use a level teaspoon for black tea, and a heaping teaspoon for oolong. Use two teaspoons for pouchong or green tea. You'll see that some teas are densely packed, so use slightly less per cup.

**Timing for the perfect cup:** steep (or brew) oolong tea, in pots for about one minute. With oolong tea in an 8 oz. cup, brew three minutes. Jasmine in an 8 oz. cup, also three minutes. For black tea in an 8 oz. cup, two to three minutes, and for loose green tea in an 8 oz. cup, three minutes. When using tea bags, follow the instruction given, but in general, brew for a half minute.

## How to Prepare a Good Cup of Tea

- The pot and cups should be warmed to help keep the temperature of the tea hotter for a longer time. To do this, pour hot water quickly over the cups and the pot.

- The quality of leaves, the temperature of the water, and the length of time the leaves are infused are important aspects of brewing a good cup of tea. The water should be about 176 - 194 degrees F (80-90 degrees C) for medium bodied tea such as Oolong; or 195 degrees F (90 degrees C) for full bodied teas such as all black teas. Use filtered water for the most pure taste.

- Choose good quality leaves and store them correctly. Leaves should be kept in an airtight clean, dry, odor-free container. Store in a cool, dry, dark place. ❑

# How to Make Your Own Tea Blends and Tea Bags

This is about taking time for yourself and having a beautiful cup of tea (no purchased tea bags please). But before you can have a cup of tea you must first choose the tea leaves. For me, that is where the fun starts. It is fun to shop Asian tea parlors or specialty tea shops for special, high-quality teas. Once I have the tea, I love to prepare my own tea blends. I usually like to start with a nice Darjeeling or another aromatic black tea and purchase it in bulk. Then I decide what flavors I would like. Sometimes I make lavender flavored tea, or rose petal, or vanilla, or lemon – the list can go on and on. I usually make enough for 5 or 6 cups – that way I am assured it will be fresh and I won't get too tired of it before I want to try something else. I store my mixture in an airtight can. When I am making tea for myself and don't want to make an entire pot, I use a tea infuser or one of my own hand-made tea bags.

I like to make gifts of my special tea blends by making my own tea bags. I package 10 or so bags in a beautiful tin box, make my own label, and give it to a special friend.

**To make your own tea bags:** you will need fine-mesh cheesecloth and thin cotton cord. Cut the cheesecloth into 2-1/2" squares. Place a heaping teaspoon of the tea blend into the center of the square. Gather the square at the top and tie a piece of thin cotton cord in a knot to secure. Be sure to leave a tail on the cord so the bag can be easily pulled from the brewing cup.

Here are three of my favorite tea blends. From left to right – black tea with rose buds, oolong tea with lavender, chamomile and green tea.

## Recipes for Tea Blends

Here are some of my favorites. The amounts of the ingredients depends upon your own personal taste. Please have fun experimenting with amounts or different ingredients.

### Lavender Tea Blend
4 parts black tea leaves
1 part organic lavender flowers

*Simply mix and store in an airtight container.*

### Rose/Vanilla Tea Blend
4 parts black tea leaves
1 part organic rose buds and petals
1 vanilla bean

*Simply mix and store in an airtight container. Remove vanilla bean after a week.*

### Lemon Earl Grey Blend
1/2 cup Earl Grey tea leaves
Zest from 1 lemon cut in very fine
  strips

*Allow zest to dry overnight. Blend zest with tea and store in an airtight container.*

### Rosemary Tea Blend
1/2 cup black tea leaves
2 tsp. fresh rosemary needles

*Simply blend and store.*

## Simplicity in Entertaining

Many of us love to entertain – but it is hard to find the time to do it right. If you order take-out, then the time-consuming cooking part of the affair is taken care of – you are left to decorate and enjoy your friends. Shown here, Asian take-out food is made extra special by adding a little ambience to the scene. It's fun to eat at a low table – a coffee table is perfect. Cover it with brown paper or some brightly colored Asian paper. You can even add a few Asian symbols to brown paper covering by using rubber stamps or cutting your own stencils. Solid colored plates work best – and be sure to give everyone chopsticks. Brew up some tea or offer Chinese or Japanese beer. Start by passing some warm damp cloths that you have heated in the microwave. End with fortune cookies. Make your own fortune cookies by purchasing some gourmet cookies. Write your own fortunes and create them on your computer or write on little slips of paper. Insert a cookie and a fortune into a clear cellophane bag, tie up with a beautiful ribbon, and enjoy the party.

# Life Affirming Plants

## Lucky Bamboo

According to Feng Shui masters, bamboo is a very powerful symbol of good fortune, wealth, and health – causing "chi" (energy) to flow better. Wherever bamboo is placed, happiness is sure to follow. In China, the plant is said to bring prosperity to a home. The plant can grow inside in vases of water or in soil. It roots very easily and can be divided and given to friends. The popular "lucky bamboo" or "prosperity bamboo" plant that is widely available today only looks like bamboo. This plant is botanically *Dracaena sanderiana*.

One of the easiest and most attractive ways of growing it is in a container filled with small pebbles to hold the stalks in place. Keep the container filled with water and the plant (and perhaps your home) will prosper. Besides the mystical properties that this plant is believed to have, it is beautiful as well. It is fast-growing, easily rooted, and the joints that occur every few inches produce shoots and leaves that are reminiscent of bamboo. It is so house-friendly – place it in every room to add a touch of the Wood element to you environment.

# Ever-Changing Hydrangea

Hydrangea is one of summer's most beautiful flowers. Hydrangea bloom in large clusters of individual flowers on bushes that are very low maintenance and controlled. The hydrangea plant gives and gives of its life and energy throughout the summer season. Hydrangeas can be blue, purple, shades of pink, or white when in full bloom. They can stay at the height of bloom for as long as a month with the colors being vibrant and true.

With the reward of large colorful blooms covering the bush that last throughout the summer, you also get a plant that changes colors as the blooms move toward the end of their season. The bloom begins its life as a green compact cluster. Upon opening, the blooms are startling shades of vivid color. As the blooms fade, so does the color. While some colors will turn a dustier color, others turn a bright green. It is fascinating to watch the coloration stages. As the blooms continue to age, they dry out and turn a rusty brown or beige with tints of pink. The blooms never fall off the bush. The dead, dry clusters should be pulled or snipped from the bush, making room for the next year's blooms.

Pictured here is a beautiful bouquet of dried hydrangea blooms. The varying colors are the result of a variety of blossom colors as well as the color stage at which the blossoms were picked for drying. The greener clusters came from blue bushes, the purple clusters from rose-colored bushes, and the bluer clusters came from purple blooms. Dried blossoms stay colorful for only about a year until they fade to brown – just in time to start drying blossoms from your new crop.

## Drying Hydrangea

Hydrangea are a great candidate for drying. The blooms remain full and whole ranging in beautiful washed and faded colors. So subtle and so beautiful. I am always fascinated at the resulting colors when the blooms are dried. My purple hydrangea dry to a beautiful blue, while my bright rose color blooms dry to a lovely lavender.

Knowing when to pick the blooms for drying is the main factor in the success of drying the blooms. To assure more colorful dried blooms, it is best to pick the fresh blooms just as they begin to fade, after the color has peaked. The flowers will feel slightly dry and stiff, yet still feel flexible. Do not pick the blooms if the flowers are soft and supple. If you pick the blooms too soon for drying, the individual flowers will curl and not dry flat. If you miss that exact time, you still have time to pick more blooms before they

104

become completely dry and colorless.
After picking the blooms there are several ways to achieve a beautiful dried cluster. If you have picked the blooms when a lot of the moisture has gone from the plant, you can simply stand them in a vase or container to dry completely. Keep them in a dry spot in your home away from direct sunlight. Allow each bloom to have plenty of air and space around them to dry, not touching other blooms. You can also hang them upside down in a cool, dry place.

There is another method I have tried with varying success. You can pick a blossom that is at the height of its life and color. Place it in a vase with just about 1/2" of water. The water is slowly absorbed into the plant, keeping it just moist enough to retain color as it begins to dry out.
*Continued on the following pages.*

## Drying Hydrangea

These blooms are almost soft and fresh, they have just begun to fade. The petals feel just slightly stiff. When dried the blooms stayed a very nice blue color. However, some of the petals curled a little, indicating too much moisture in the petals.

This is the next stage in the purple hydrangea's life. The bloom is faded from its most vibrant purple color. When dried this will be a very beautiful lavender blue color, with all the individual flower petals being flat and unchanged.

These blooms have faded from bright blue to this green color. When I dried these blooms at this stage, the cluster dried to a light green/beige color. I picked some blooms just as they were turning from bright blue to a slightly more green color. I had good success with the drying – the cluster resulted in a faded blue color.

These blooms were once a vibrant purple color at the height of the blooming season. When dried the blooms are a very pale beige/lavender with deeper lavender on the tips of flowers.

# Firelight & Energy

The fire of the sun gives energy. When this burning heat is brought into a room, it creates an atmosphere charged with power. We think of colors such as orange and red and the heat of summer or tropical climes.

# Bringing Fire Into Your Environment

There are many ways we can introduce this element into our décor.

Sunlight
Candles
Crystals
Sunflower Pattern
Incense
Gold Leafing
Lumineria
Bright Colored Silks
Fireplace

## Cozy Dining Room

The fire in the fireplace adds the energetic spark that this room needs to balance the overwhelming Earth and Wood elements that impart strength, comfort, and tranquility to the ambience. The wood stained walls and furniture surround the occupants with Wood energy. The Earth element is represented by the stone fireplace, the earthtone colors, pumpkins, and the pottery serving pieces. The curved chair and other curved shapes introduce a characteristic of the Water element. Metal accessories such as the brass candlesticks on the table and the copper kettle on the mantle add the balance of the Metal element.

# Parchment Lanterns to Make

With heavyweight parchment paper and roller-type rubber stamps, it's easy to create exquisite candle collars that diffuse the candlelight and create a glowing lantern. These trimmed collars are quick and inexpensive to create – fill the table with them for a striking arrangement. Designed by Marie Browning from her book, *Crafting with Vellum and Parchment,* published by Sterling Publishing Co., NY, NY.

**Supplies**

White parchment paper
Rubber stamps or roller-type rubber stamp
Embossing power
Double-sided tape
Scissors
Glass votive candle holder
Votive candles
Candle base (optional)

**Here's How**

1. Cut a parchment rectangle that, when rolled into a cylinder shape, will fit around your candleholder. Make sure it is higher than the glass votive holder.

2. Decorate by embossing. Load a roller stamp with thermal embossing ink and roll along the one edge of the parchment paper. Sprinkle on gold embossing powder and heat to set.

3. After decorating, form the parchment into cylinders and adhere with double-sided tape. Place it over the votive holder.

4. (Optional) Place the candle lantern on a low dish or other heat-proof surface to complete the effect.

*Caution:* Never leave lanterns unattended. ❏

# Japanese Lantern

This simple lantern, made to fit a metal candle holder, is decorated with roller rubber stamps. Use a roller-type stamp with Asian characters and lighter-colored ink to create the stripes of symbols in the background. Use a bamboo design stamp with black ink to create the main motif. Designed by Marie Browning from her book, *Crafting with Vellum and Parchment,* published by Sterling Publishing Co., NY, NY.

## Supplies

Red parchment paper
Rubber stamps or roller-type rubber stamp
Gold and black ink
Double-sided tape
Craft knife
Decorative scissors (deckle design used)
Glass votive candle holder
Votive candles
Candle base (optional)

## Here's How

1. Determine the circumference of the candle stand and add 1/2" to the circumference measurement. Determine the height you wish the lantern to be. You can make the lantern any height you desire, depending upon the size of your stand. Draw a rectangle for your lantern measurements on parchment with a white pencil or crayon.

2. Stamp the stripes of symbols all across the piece of parchment using gold ink, with the stripes going vertical.

3. Stamp the bamboo motifs around the lamp with black, varying the heights.

4. Cut along the marked lines on the bottom and sides with a craft knife. Cut the top edge with the decorative scissors.

5. Roll the parchment in a cylinder shape and secure with double-sided tape. Place parchment cylinder in the stand and place candle in center.

*Caution:* Never leave lanterns unattended. ❑

# Meditation Center

Make your home a sanctuary, a refuge that envelopes and protects you at the end of the day. Set aside a place within your home where you can go for a quiet moment. Whether you meditate or just close your eyes and rest for a few minutes – this time with only yourself – without noise or disruptions is very important. When meditating, I find it helpful to have something on which I can focus. In using a physical item to center my thoughts, I am more able to free my mind of all other things and start to gain serenity. Here is a meditation center that is easy to put together from various types of decorated candles. The Asian design of this ensemble is esthetically pleasing and adds a touch of the exotic. The designs on the large candle in the center were added with a decal. The symbols on the small square candles were carved into the wax then painted with gold metallic paint. The symbols on the container candle were painted onto a piece of parchment that was wrapped around the glass container.

The candles are placed in a teak wood tray. The space between the candles are filled in with smooth pebbles. Notice that this meditation center contains all the earth elements. The candles represent the fire element. The tray brings the strength and stability of the wood element. The stones are the earth element. The metal element comes from the Chinese coin and other metal trim. The glass square adds the balance of the water element.

To enjoy your meditation session, sit in a quiet room of a comfortable temperature. Place your meditation center in front of you. Light the candles and focus on the flames to begin clearing your mind and helping you to relax. The flames also help cleanse the atmosphere. Try to not think. If your mind starts to capture a thought, try to dispel it and think only of the firelight and allow no other notion to take over. ❏

# Aromatherapy

Burning a candle or incense energizes a home by introducing fire energy – cleansing and purifying the atmosphere. Candles, incense, soaps, and other bath products can be powerful vehicles for aromatherapy. All these items can be made for pennies at home. And it is much easier than you would imagine to makes your own soaps, candles, bath gel, bath salts, or air freshener.

## Essential Oils

When essential oils are used in the making of these products, you will gain healthful benefits. Essential oils from plants have a mysterious effect on the body. Pure oil aromas allow the body and the mind to renew harmony and well-being. The distillation process involves fire relieving the plant of its oils. When we inhale this pure essence, the plant releases its benefits to us and we discover our link with nature. A note of caution – essential oils are highly concentrated and must be diluted before they can be safely applied to the skin or blended into soaps (1% or less is considered to be a safe level for soapmaking). Too much essential oil can cause severe skin irritations. People with sensitive skin or allergies should be careful when using essential oils in their soap.

**Effects of Aromas**
Each essential oil scent has a different effect. While no medical claims can be made, it is believed that essential oils affect us emotionally, physically, and aesthetically. It is not a surprise that a scented bath can soothe us and renew our spirits.
- Peaceful and relaxing scents - lavender, sandalwood, chamomile, rose, lemon verbena.
- Energizing - rosemary, peppermint, jasmine, honey
- Uplifting - orange, rosemary, sage, pine
- Focusing - grapefruit, cinnamon, chamomile, lavender, orange, ylang ylang

## A Therapeutic Bath

A fragrant bath is a perfect way to improve your mood. A bath engages almost all the senses, allowing you to respond to visual, olfactory, tactile, thermal, and auditory cues. Try adding other sensory experiences to the bath ritual such as fragrant bubbles, ocean sounds, or candlelight to aid relaxation. Here are some recipes for a perfect bath.
- To relax before bedtime, draw a warm bath (not hot because it can dry out the skin). Light some candles or incense in calming scents. This will help you slip into a tranquil, restful sleep.
- At the end of a work day, a stimulating, cool bath increases circulation and refreshes. Use fresh herbal scents to soothe tired muscles.
- Uplift your psyche with energizing citrus and honey scents. Add sounds of the ocean and fun bubbles.
- For a romantic evening, draw a warm bath, add classical music and warm, sensual scents. Place a vase of fresh roses in the room and add some rose petals to the tub.

## Make Your Own Bath Products
- Making bath salts or bath oils is easy. You can purchase the bases needed such as plain bath crystals or plain bath oil at many craft shops. Add the fragrance of your choice, and tint the bath salts or oil if desired with soap tints. You can even add a bit of botanical materials such as lavender or dried rose petals. Mix and put in a pretty jar – ready to add to a bath.
- Make your own soap. There are many books and kits available that will give explicit instructions for this engaging and addicting craft. In many craft shops you can find soap bases, molds, fragrance oils and coloring. Most soap bases can be melted in a microwave and then poured into a mold to harden. The fun part is choosing botanical items to add to the soap such as oatmeal for its cleansing power, lavender for its beauty and fragrance, cinnamon to create an astringent – the list goes on and on. Experiment and choose your own personal preferences.

## Making Your Own Candles

Simply put, all you need to make your own candles are wax, a cotton wick, a container to melt the wax in, and a mold or a glass container for the candle. The process is simple as well – after you have prepared the glass container or mold, melt the wax and pour it into the mold or container. Let it harden and it is done. Of course, there are a few other precautions and details you need to know. There are many books, candle making supplies, and even candle-making kits available to make it easy for you to create your own beautiful candles.

## What You Need

Candle wax; soy wax is now available for those concerned about our renewable resources
Fragrance oil • Coloring • Candle wicking
Pourable metal container for melting wax
Candle thermometer • Mold or a glass container

## Here's How

1. Prepare mold by securing the wick in place. Instructions will be included with the mold. You can choose to make a candle in a clear glass container so the candle burns right in the container. A wick tab is needed to weight and secure the wick to the bottom of the container. The tab is put at the bottom of the wick and the top of the wick is tied to a dowel that spans the top of the container. This suspends the wick into the container.
2. Melt the candle wax slowly in a metal container that is placed into a larger pan of water (creating a type of double boiler). Place the thermometer in the pouring container. Heat the wax to 180 degrees F. Add scent and coloration. Stir to mix. Bring wax to the proper temperature for the mold you are using. For most candle molds such as acrylic and metal, bring the wax to 190-200 degrees F. If using a glass container, wax should be 180 degrees F. DO NOT LEAVE WAX UNATTENDED, AND DO NOT HEAT WAX OVER 210 DEGREES F.
3. Pour into mold. And allow to harden. Wax will shrink and form a depression. Refill this depression with additional melted wax. Allow to harden.
4. Remove candle from mold. Or, if using a glass container, simply cut wick at dowel to remove dowel and your candle is complete. ❏

# Earthy
# Elements

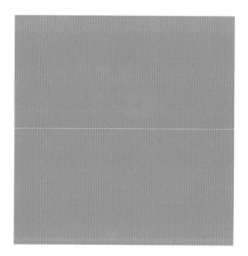

## Pottery and Pumpkins

Items such as pottery, terra cotta, mosaics, bricks, root vegetables, pumpkins, create an atmosphere that says "I'm home, I'm comfortable, I'm centered."

Pottery vessels, especially grouped together, are beautiful decorative accessories. The shapes, colors, and textures appeal to our esthetics and harken back to a simpler time. Because pottery vessels have been used in every culture throughout time, you can find many different styles available to suit your decor. Early American salt glazed pots and vessels are especially desired as collectibles. Italian olive crocks and oil pitchers are beautifully earthy in their colors and textures and are quite useful as well. Asian crocks can be rough and primitive or smooth, delicate, and highly decorated.

A display of gourds and pumpkins is a beautiful sight. The orange, ochre and yellow colors; the rounded and curved shapes; and the incredible tactile surfaces make these items more art than vegetable. Shown on the opposite page, this homeowner has created a fall display on her porch. She has lined an old wheelbarrow with colorful leaves, then piled in every kind of gourd and pumpkin she could find. An arrangement of dried pods, leaves, and other material placed at the back of the gourds complete the scene. This porch says "welcome" to all passersby.

122

# Mosaic Bowl

This earthy bowl was easy to create using a pre-form mosaic technique. The bowl can be handy in the kitchen to display fruit or vegetables or even used outdoors. You'll be surprised at how easy the technique is. It's fun to save up broken pottery to create unique gifts for friends. Designed by Connie Sheerin, from her book, *Mosaics in an Afternoon*, published by Sterling, Publishing. Co, NY, NY.

## Supplies

8" clay saucer
Grout
Broken pottery and ceramic tiles
Mastic or thick white glue

## Here's How

1. Plan the design and choose enough pieces of broken pottery to cover the bottom surface and enough square tiles to be used as two rows of border around rim of the saucer.
2. Glue the pieces of tile and pottery to the saucer and allow to dry.
3. Mix the grout with water to a consistency of cooked oatmeal. Spread grout over the pieces and work into the spaces between the pottery and tile. Wipe with a damp cloth to smooth the grout, removing the grout from the surface of the tiles and pottery. Continue wiping and finish by polishing the surface of the pieces with a soft cloth. Allow grout to dry. ❏

## Pebbles & Pods

Displays of pebbles or seeds and pods can be both beautiful and beneficial as promoting earth energy. Shown on this page, a collection of pebbles collected from various parts of the world are displayed in a hand-turned bowl of ash created by artist, Roger Foster. The collection of seeds, pods, dried fungi, and balls of twined reed make an interesting collection in an antique wooden dough bowl, which belonged to my husband's grandmother.

# Flowing Water

The force of flowing water is mighty. When water energy is used in your garden or inside your home it can promote spirituality, quiet and tranquility.

## Natural Baths

Water energy is found most predominantly in the bathroom and kitchen. Because of the metal faucets and the glazed ceramic fixtures, the spaces can sometimes seem too sleek and cold. Shown in the photos, this bathroom at Whispering Waters bed and breakfast is an example of how this space was warmed up with natural, earthy elements. Here, pebbles were used to create a floor in a shower and a backsplash around a tub. The technique was done like the mosaic technique described in the previous chapter entitled "Earthy Elements." Notice the tinted and polished plaster walls – these also extend the earthy appeal.

# Make a Clay Indoor Fountain

This rustic fountain would make a nice patio, porch, or sunroom fountain – or bring this outdoor look inside to the kitchen or family room. It has an earthy attractiveness that evokes an image of a country French chateau. Mossy plants work well for this look. *Designed by Rhonda Garson.*

**Pump:** Small fountain submersible pump with outlet on top; 60 GPH @ 1 foot is more than enough performance

**Tubing:** Flexible plastic tubing to fit the largest outlet on your pump, 12" length

**Pump Housing:** Two pieces of plastic foam (NOT florist's foam!), any color, 12" square x 1/2" to 1" thick. This will be used to create a space for the pump.

**Base Container:** Round clay pot with no drain hole, 10" diam. x 7" deep (inside must be sealed so it will be watertight)

**Top Container:** Round clay pot WITH drain hole, 6-1/2" diam. x 4" deep (does not need to be sealed). Hole can be drilled to accommodate tubing if it does not have a hole.

**Filler:** Small and medium stones; Bag of natural stone aquarium gravel

**Sealants:** Sealant for waterproofing (such as epoxy resin); Plumber's Putty, smallest container you can buy

**Tools:** Serrated kitchen knife

## Here's How

1. Measure the diameter of your larger pot approximately 2-1/2" below the rim. Cut a circle from one of the 12" sq. pieces of plastic foam to this dimension. (Save your scraps; they will be used later.) Cut six equally spaced drainage holes, each slightly larger than a dime, around the perimeter of the foam circle about 3/4" in from the edge. Also cut a notch for the electric cord. Place this circle in the large pot. The top of the circle should be about 2-1/2" below the top of the pot. This foam circle does not need to be watertight, just secure enough to hold up the other pot. Some of the discarded foam can be used as wedges under the foam circle to give it more strength and stability.

2. Make sure the drainage hole in the small pot is large enough to accommodate the plastic tubing. Ream out the hole with a drill if it is not.

3. Temporarily position the smaller pot on top of this foam circle. Place it so that it is off-set (not centered) and against the position where the electric cord comes out. The top pot should be about 3/4" from the edge of the large pot. With a pencil, mark the position of the small pot's drainage hole on the plastic foam. Remove the smaller pot and the foam circle.

4. Cut a hole in the plastic foam where you marked. Cut it large enough to accommodate the plastic tubing. This joint does not need to be watertight.

5. Place your pump in the bottom of the larger pot. Position the pump outflow post so that it will approximately line up with the tubing hole you cut in the foam circle. Place the plastic tubing on the pump outlet. Run the tubing through the tubing hole in the foam circle and position the plastic foam in the 10" pot.

6. Measure the inside diameter of the 6-1/2" pot approximately 1" below the rim. Cut a second plastic foam circle to this dimension from the other piece of foam. (Again, save those scraps.) Cut a hole in the center of this circle just barely larger than the diameter of the plastic tubing. This should be a snug fit. If too loose, you can fill in the gap with plumber's putty after final positioning of the circle in the pot. Do a dry fit only now and remove the circle.

7. Run the tubing through the hole in the bottom of the smaller pot. Now place the smaller pot on top of the plastic foam circle in the 10" pot. Slightly tilt the smaller pot away from the near edge (this will be the back edge) of the larger pot by putting a thin scrap of plastic foam under the back edge of the smaller pot. This will cause the water to overflow the smaller pot on the front edge

only. Run the tubing through the smaller foam circle. Position the foam circle inside the smaller pot approximately 1" below the rim.

8. The joint between the plastic foam and the clay pot must be watertight, so seal the edge between the two with plumber's putty. Run a moistened finger over the plumber's putty for a smooth joint.

9. Cut the tubing flush with the top of the pot.

10. Stack some of the larger stones toward the back of the top pot behind the tubing. Place other stones around the tubing so that the stones slope slightly from back to front. Fill in any gaps with the aquarium gravel. (Be careful not to get any of the gravel down the plastic tubing.) The stones should be slightly higher than the tubing in the back and flush with it in the front. Only the opening of the tubing should be visible.

11. Pour water into the bottom pot through the drainage holes in the foam circle. Be sure the pump is fully submerged.

12. Fill the area between the two pots with the scraps of plastic foam about halfway up to the rim. This is to make the fountain a bit lighter. Do not block the drainage holes in the circle.

13. Cover the plastic foam pieces with stones. After positioning the larger stones, fill in any small gaps with smaller stones and aquarium gravel. If desired, add some sheet moss for decoration.

14. If the water is coming out of the tubing too quickly, adjust the flow control on the pump. (Some disassembly and reassembly will be required.) You may also experiment with the placement of the rocks to get the best sound. ❑

# Make a Pottery and Pebble Fountain

The sleekness of the finish on the containers and design feature, the globe-shaped forms, and the soothing running water all make this an exceptionally tranquil fountain. And the designer was exceptionally clever – who would believe that the top globe is a round salt shaker. The water pushes through the holes in the shaker, creating wonderful spouts of water. The spouting water fills up the first plate of stones, then cascades down the sides to the stone-filled base container. You can adjust the pump to your preference for the height of the water spout. All will be in harmony when this fountain is the focal point of an Asian inspired space. *Designed by Patty Cox.*

**Pump:** Submersible water pump for fountain

**Tubing:** 3/8" tubing

**Pump Housing:** Round shiny, black-glazed ceramic bowl, 5" diam.

**Container:** Black glazed ceramic square platter, 13" square

**Design Feature:**
Black square plate, 8" (matches platter);
Round salt shaker, 2-1/2" diam.

**Hardware:** Five H-clips (plywood spacers)

**Filler:** Black Mexican beach pebbles, large and small; Two bags black glass half marbles;

**Plants:** Small potted plants, *(optional)*

**Sealant:** Epoxy glue

**Tools:** Mini drill with 1/16" diamond bit and silicone carbide grinding stone bit

## Instructions

### Pump Housing:

1. Drill a 3/8" hole in the center bottom of the 5" bowl.
2. Glue five H-clips around lip of bowl with epoxy glue. This will lift the bowl off the base enough so that water can circulate.

### Top Platform:

3. Drill a 3/8" hole in center of the 8" square plate.
4. Glue plate on inverted bowl base, aligning holes.
5. Thread tubing through inverted bowl (housing) and plate center holes. Arrange pump under bowl housing. Trim lower end of tubing to fit on pump. Detach tubing from pump for now.
6. Work salt shaker over top end of tubing, so that it will rest on plate.

### Platter Container:

7. Arrange pump in center (the deepest) portion of platter. Attach tubing to pump and place bowl/plate/salt shaker structure over pump.
8. Fill platter with water. Plug in pump to test workings. When it is working correctly continue to finish fountain.
9. Arrange rocks around plate-table and around bowl in platter. ❏

# Decorative Projects & Techniques

*Pictured at right:* Asian Wall Scroll, see instructions on page 138.

# Asian Wall Scroll

*Pictured on previous page.*

Made of paper and using rubber stamps, this exotic scroll would make a wonderful addition to an entry. Choose an Asian symbol from the patterns included to wish your visitors well. *Designed by Marci Donley.*

## Supplies

Asian design paper, 13" x 25" for background
3/8" dowels cut into 2 pieces, each 14-1/2" long
4, 1" wooden balls with holes, for ends of dowels
Metallic gold paint
White charcoal paper, 18" x 8"
Heavy vellum paper 6-1/2" x 7-1/2"
Asian symbol stamps
Gold pigment ink pad
Embossing powder (optional)
Sepia ink
Brush
Cord for hanging, 1yd.
Glue
Craft knife
Ruler

## Here's How

1. On the background paper, measure and mark areas for mounting to dowels. Along the 13" side (top and bottom of paper) measure and mark 1" from edge, then 2-1/2" from edge. Make marks on the backside of the paper.

2. In the space between the marks, you will need to cut out three squares. See Fig. 1 showing measurements for cutting.

3. Paint the dowels and balls with the metallic gold paint. Let dry.

4. On the white 18" x 8" piece of paper, stamp long vertical rows of the Asian symbols using the gold ink. Use embossing powder if desired.

5. Use a tissue to rub some gold ink on the paper to make it look antique.

6. Trim 1/2" off each side of this piece of paper to make it look neater. Cut piece of paper into two pieces, measuring 17" x 4" and 17" x 3".

7. Glue these two strips to the background paper with approx. 2" margin between.

8. Choose an Asian symbol pattern from the following pages. Enlarge symbol if desired. Place the vellum paper over the symbol and paint the design onto the vellum with the brush and sepia ink. Glue this piece to the front of the scroll as shown.

9. To make a pocket for the dowel. Fold down the 1" strip at each end of background paper, and glue it to the back of the piece directly below the cutout area. Allow glue to dry and slide dowels in place.

10. Attach cord to the top dowel for hanging. ❑

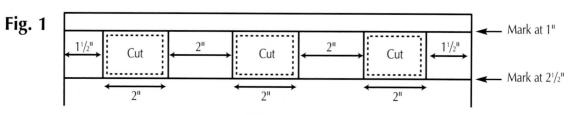

**Fig. 1**

1¹/₂"  Cut  2"  Cut  2"  Cut  1¹/₂"  ← Mark at 1"

2"  2"  2"  ← Mark at 2¹/₂"

## Tranquility Symbol - AN

## Harmony Symbol - HE

## Joy Symbol - HIS

## Wisdom Symbol - SHI

# Framed Nature

These framed pressed leaves are designed to sit in the window so they will be backlit. The leaves are sandwiched between vellum panels, one or two leaves per panel, then the panels are layered, one atop the other. The following instructions are for the smaller frame. For the large piece, use a larger frame with divided panels. Two vellum panels are made to fit frame. One panel has skeleton leaves and the other panel has the three pressed darker leaves and a pressed fern piece. Designed by Marie Browning, from her book, *Crafting with Vellum & Parchment*, published by Sterling Publishing, Co., NY, NY.

## Supplies

Flat wooden frame with 5" x 7" opening
2 pieces clear glass, each 5" x 7"
6 pieces frosted vellum (two for each panel), each 5" x 7"
Pressed leaves and fern
Silicon glue
white acrylic craft paint
Sponge brush
Sandpaper

## Here's How

1. Paint the frame with acrylic paint and allow to dry.
2. Sand frame to achieve a worn, white-washed look.
3. Place on piece of glass in the frame.
4. Construct the vellum panels: Place one piece of vellum on surface. Put one or two leaves on vellum and secure leaf with a tiny dot of silicon glue. Place other piece of vellum on top. Secure vellum pieces to one another with a couple of dots of glue along each edge. Continue making two more panels.
5. Layer the vellum panels in the frame and top with the second piece of glass. Secure glass in frame. ❏

# How to Stamp with Paint

Stamping with large decorator foam stamps makes it easy to create decorative accessories for your home.

## Supplies

Foam stamp
Acrylic craft paint
Foam brush, roller, or applicator
Surface

## Here's How

1. Apply paint to the stamp smoothly using a roller, brush, or applicator.
2. Press stamp down onto surface and walk your fingers around back of stamp to apply pressure.
3. Lift stamp straight up.

You can get 2 or 3 pressings from one paint application.

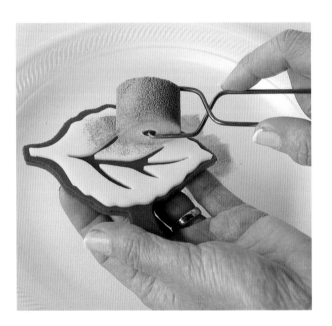

# Stamped Ivy Ensemble

## Rubber Stamped Flower Pot

*Designed by Marci Donley.*

## Supplies

Terra cotta pot
Satin finish wall paint, linen color
Sage green acrylic craft paint
Neutral glazing medium
1" foam brush
Wall combing tool
Vine design rubber stamp
Green ink pad
Metallic gold paint marker
Clear gloss sealer

## Here's How

1. Apply linen colored wall paint to pot. Let dry.
2. Mix a small amount of sage green paint with an equal amount of neutral glazing medium.
3. Paint the pot with this mixture.
4. While glaze is still wet, use the wall combing tool to create a vertical pattern on pot. Let dry.
5. Stamp the green vine design on the pot.
6. Add some gold dots with the metallic marker for interest and contrast.
7. Allow project to dry overnight. Apply two coats of gloss sealer. ❏

# Stool, Tray, and Photo Frame
*Designed by Marci Donley.*

## Supplies
Wooden surface
Sandpaper
Satin finish wall paint, linen color
Acrylic craft paint: sage green, brown, teal, ivy green, mushroom, rose, metallic bronze
Clear glazing medium
Ivy foam stamps in 3-4 sizes
Butterfly foam stamp (for tray only)
2" paint brush
Sponge applicator
Liner brush
Clear gloss sealer

## Here's How
1. Sand the surface to smooth it. Wipe off dust.
2. Apply a coat of linen colored paint to surface and allow to dry.
3. Mix the sage green paint with glazing medium to create a translucent color, mixing about 3 tablespoons of color with an equal amount of glazing medium.
4. Using the 4" brush and the sage green glaze, paint the surface, leaving brush strokes visible to add texture.
5. Trim the edges of the tray and stool, and the outside edge of frame using metallic bronze paint.
6. Trim the inside edge of the frame using rose paint.
7. Apply green, brown, teal, and ivy green paint to the surface of the ivy foam stamp shapes. Stamp the designs onto the surface. Use the various sizes of stamps and colors of paint to create a flowing pattern with random colors of leaves. More than one color of paint can be applied to each leaf stamp at one time.
8. Using the liner brush and brown paint, paint in vein lines and vines.
9. Allow project to dry thoroughly. Then seal with two coats of sealer. ❑

# Stamped Leaves & Fern

From wall hangings to furniture, there is no limit to what you can decorate with foam stamp designs. This chest of drawers and framed fern prints have been created using paint and foam stamps. See page 144 for instructions for the stamping technique. *Designed by Kathi Bailey for Plaid Enterprises, Inc.*

## Chest of Drawers

**Supplies**

Satin finish wall paint, white
Green acrylic craft paint
Neutral glazing medium
Foam stamp leaf designs, two different ones used
2" brush
Foam applicator
Clear acrylic sealer

**Here's How**

1. Prepare surface of chest. Paint with several coats of white paint until adequately covered. Let dry.
2. Mix a small amount of green paint with an equal amount of neutral glazing medium. Using the brush, apply this to the edge of chest top and the drawer knobs. Allow to dry.
3. Apply green paint to the foam stamps and decorate chest as desired. Let dry.
4. Apply sealer to chest for protection. ❏

## Framed Fern Prints

**Supplies**

Frame, size of your choice (8" x 10" and 5" x 7" sizes used)
Handmade paper, cut to fit into frame
Foam stamp in fern design
Green acrylic craft paint
Foam applicator

**Here's How**

1. Apply the green paint to the fern stamp and apply to handmade paper pieces as desired.
2. Secure prints in frame. ❏

# How to Stencil

Stenciling can be used to decorate furniture, walls, ceilings. floors – and even used outdoors on stepping stones as this project shows. Here's how to use stenciling to decorate a variety of household surfaces.

## Supplies

Pre-cut stencil of your choice

Stencil paint colors, or acrylic craft paint

Stencil brush, one for each color used, 1/2" size is a good universal size

Palette or disposal foam plates

Masking tape

Paper towels

**Photo 1**

**Photo 2**

### Here's How

1. Choose the stencil and the colors you desire for your project.
2. Prepare the surface of your project.
3. Tape stencil in place on project.
4. Squeeze out a small amount of paint onto the palette or onto a disposable plate.
5. Load brush by dabbing it up and down into paint. *See photo 2.*

**Photo 3**

**Photo 4**

6. Dab brush on a paper towel to remove most of the paint and to disperse paint evenly with brush. Stenciling is done with a nearly dry brush so don't leave any wet-looking paint in brush. *See photo 3.*
7. Begin applying paint to cutout areas of stencil. Place brush just outside of the area and begin moving brush in a circular motion as you move it into the cutout area. Move the brush around the design. Apply the paint darker on the outer edges of the design. *See photo 4.* ❏

Stenciling was used to decorate cement stepping stones. Plain stepping stones are available at most home improvement centers. Use outdoor paint to do the stenciling. *Designed by Susan Goans Driggers from her book FLOOR STYLE, published by Sterling Publishing Co., NY, NY.*

VIVIAN RUSSELL
EDITH WHARTON'S ITALIAN GARDENS

# How to Crackle

You can give your furniture pieces the look of age and history by using crackling medium. There are two methods for creating crackled finishes.

## Method 1: Two-Color Crackled Finish

**Supplies**
Crackle Medium
Two contrasting colors of flat latex paint
Foam brush

**Here's How**
1. Prepare surface being painted.
2. Apply one color of paint to surface. It doesn't matter if you put the light color as the bottom coat or the dark color – it depends upon the effect you wish to create. For this method, the cracks will be the color of this basecoat. Allow paint to dry.
3. Using a foam brush, apply a thick coat of crackling medium to surface. Do not brush over the medium but apply even coats. Allow to dry.
4. Apply a second coat of paint. If you are applying the light color as the top color, you will need to apply a thick coat of paint. As the paint dries cracks will form. Let dry completely.
5. Optional: protect with a varnish or sealer.

## Method 2: Antiqued Crackled Finish

**Supplies**
Crackle Medium
Two contrasting colors of flat latex paint
Neutral glazing medium
Foam brush
Smooth sponge
Clear brush-on acrylic sealer

**Here's How**
1. Prepare surface.
2. Paint the surface with the lighter shade of paint. Apply two to three coats for complete coverage. Let dry completely overnight.
3. Apply a thick coat of crackle medium to the piece. Do not brush over the medium. *See photo 1.* Let dry.
4. Apply a thick coat of brush-on acrylic varnish. As it dries cracks will form. Let dry completely.
5. Mix the dark color of paint with an equal amount of neutral glazing medium to create an antiquing stain.
6. Using a sponge, rub antiquing onto the surface and into cracks of project. Let dry. *See Photo 2.*
7. Optional: apply another coat of sealer for protection. ❏

Photo 1

Photo 2

Photo courtesy of
Plaid Enterprises, Inc.

# Asian Symbols Slate and Napkin

Decorating with Asian symbols is exotic and mysterious – not to mention the artistry of each of the symbols. Here are two projects you can create using the patterns given for the symbols. The napkin requires that you make your own foam stamp, and the hanging slate is created with a stencil template hand-cut from foam. *Designed by Jean Henrich.*

## Raised Design Slate

**Supplies**

1 sheet of thin craft foam
Craft knife
Repostionable glue
Hanging slate piece
Black acrylic paint and round artist brush
Sheet rock compound
Squeegee
Acrylic sealer

**Here's How**

1. Make a copy of one of the characters of your choice.
2. Place a small amount of repositionable glue onto the back of the copy. Place the copy onto the sheet of thin craft foam.
3. Use the craft knife to cut out the character from the craft foam, creating a stencil.
4. Apply repositionable glue onto the back of the stencil and position it onto the slate.
5. Use a squeegee to spread the sheet rock compound over the stencil design. Allow to dry until the compound is dry to the touch.
6. Carefully peel back the foam stencil. Let the compound dry completely.
7. Use the craft knife to scrape away and remove any unwanted sheet rock compound from the slate.
8. Seal the sheet with sealer and let dry.
9. Paint the symbol with the black acrylic paint. Let dry.
10. Reapply sealer to the symbol. ❏

## Stamped Napkin

**Supplies**

1 sheet of thin craft foam
1 sheet of 1/4" thick craft foam
Craft knife
Repositionable glue
Acrylic craft paint plus fabric medium
Foam applicator
Fabric item of your choice (napkin shown)

**Here's How**

1. Make a copy of one of the characters of your choice.
2. Place a small amount of repositionable glue onto the back of the copy. Place the copy onto the sheet of thin craft foam.
3. Use the craft knife to cut out the character from the craft foam. You will be using the cut out pieces of the design.
4. Cut a square of thick craft foam just slightly bigger than the symbol.

5. Apply repositionable glue to the *front* of the symbol. Attach the symbol to the thick square of foam, creating a stamp with the symbol in reverse. (When it is stamped, it will be the right way.) Use the original template to help you arrange the shapes correctly.

6. Mix acrylic paint with a fabric medium 50/50 ratio. Use a foam applicator to apply the paint evenly to the surface of the foam stamp. Press the stamp onto the surface of fabric. ❏

# Windchimes Plant Stake

Windchimes help to slow down the flow of energy and have a calming effect. Here is a windchime that can be poked into a plant or in your garden to supply a tinkling symphony. *Designed by Jean Henrich.*

## Supplies

1 - 3/8" x 36" round zinc rod
5 - 3/8" wind chime pipes
Assortment of glass beads
7 small eye hooks
Drill with 1/16" bit
Wood glue
Metallic blue acrylic craft paint
Outdoor sealer
Jute cord (thin beading variety)
Decorative wooden knob
Wooden disk, 3" diameter, 1/2" thick, with 3/8" hole in center.
3 small, thin (1/8" or 1/16" thick) wood pieces
Silk ribbon (optional)

## Here's How

1. Drill 5 small holes around the edge of the wooden disk, spaced evenly, for the wind chime pipes. Drill three more holes as shown by the "X" marks on Fig. 1, for the strung beads.
2. Glue the wooden knob on top of the wooden disk. Let dry.
3. Paint the wooden piece as well as the small, thin wooden pieces. Let dry and seal with outdoor sealer.
4. Screw the eye hooks into all the drilled holes.
5. Cut equal lengths of jute and string through the holes in the wind chimes. Slide a bead down the strands of jute. Then knot the ends of the jute onto the eye hooks.
6. Drill small holes at one end of each of the thin wood pieces.
7. Cut three lengths of jute ranging from 7" to 12". Tie a wooden piece on the end of each jute length. Make a knot about 1" above this wooden piece, then slide a bead down to the knot. Continue knotting and sliding beads down jute cord. End with a knot above the last bead. Tie the end of the jute to the eye hook.
8. Place wood glue into the center hole of the wooden disk and position zinc rod in hole. Let glue dry.
9. Decorate the top of the knob with silk ribbons if desired. ❑

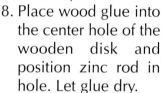

**Fig. 2**

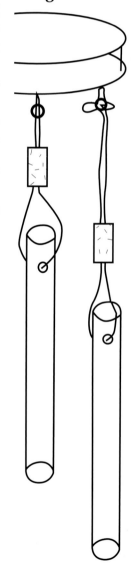

**Fig. 1**

# Metric Conversion Chart

## Inches to Millimeters and Centimeters

| Inches | MM | CM |
|---|---|---|
| 1/8 | 3 | .3 |
| 1/4 | 6 | .6 |
| 3/8 | 10 | 1.0 |
| 1/2 | 13 | 1.3 |
| 5/8 | 16 | 1.6 |
| 3/4 | 19 | 1.9 |
| 7/8 | 22 | 2.2 |
| 1 | 25 | 2.5 |
| 1-1/4 | 32 | 3.2 |
| 1-1/2 | 38 | 3.8 |
| 1-3/4 | 44 | 4.4 |
| 2 | 51 | 5.1 |
| 3 | 76 | 7.6 |
| 4 | 102 | 10.2 |
| 5 | 127 | 12.7 |
| 6 | 152 | 15.2 |
| 7 | 178 | 17.8 |
| 8 | 203 | 20.3 |
| 9 | 229 | 22.9 |
| 10 | 254 | 25.4 |
| 11 | 279 | 27.9 |
| 12 | 305 | 30.5 |

## Yards to Meters

| Yards | Meters |
|---|---|
| 1/8 | .11 |
| 1/4 | .23 |
| 3/8 | .34 |
| 1/2 | .46 |
| 5/8 | .57 |
| 3/4 | .69 |
| 7/8 | .80 |
| 1 | .91 |
| 2 | 1.83 |
| 3 | 2.74 |
| 4 | 3.66 |
| 5 | 4.57 |
| 6 | 5.49 |
| 7 | 6.40 |
| 8 | 7.32 |
| 9 | 8.23 |
| 10 | 9.14 |

# Index